Birthing Fire

Meditations

on

the

Sacred Feminine

Marlaina Donato

Ekstasis Multimedia
Blairstown, New Jersey

Ekstasis Multimedia: http://www.booksandbrush.net

ISBN-13: 978-0615717340
ISBN-10: 0615717349

Table of Contents

For Jennifer O'Hagan, Goddess of Healing;

Thank you for changing my health and my life

with your knowledge and friendship.

And for Lightning Hawk, Spirit Elder and Beloved Teacher;

Thank you for guiding me through the labyrinth.

Preface

The feminine creative force of Deity has been called *Goddess, Divine Mother, Sacred Feminine, Mother Nature, Mary Mother of God,* and the *One of Ten Thousand Names.* Early matriarchal cultures worshipped a supreme Mother Goddess, and women's wisdom and knowledge of birth, death, healing, and prophesy were revered. As time moved on, the influence of patriarchal invaders spread and eventually conquered these early peaceful Goddess-honoring societies. Male deities took preference in worship, but it was women who often tended the oracles of the Greek gods Apollo, Dionysos, and Zeus. However, many sacred practices were forced underground when women's mysticism was seen as a threat. As orthodox religion demonized direct communion with Deity and churches replaced the sacred ground of the wilderness, all yearnings for spiritual ecstasy was labeled as sin. During the holocaust of the Inquisition, woman who was once seen as the embodiment of the Great Goddess of Creation and who was once the spiritual cohesive of ancient society was stripped down to a creature not even worthy of a soul.

No one remembered—or was allowed to remember—the early years of Christianity when women were priests; they baptized, instructed, and blessed. No one remembered they were prophets, writers, and dedicated followers of Christ. The established church opposed Christian Gnostic sects that believed in the Trinity of Father, *Mother, and* Son.

It is difficult to imagine that women were once believed to be soulless when we glimpse the unhindered female spirit—a mother's sunlit eyes, a little girl dancing, a grandmother sharing a memory, a young woman passionate about her work, or a woman joyfully in love. When we see the shimmering souls of other women, we are able to glimpse the Authentic Woman within and have the courage to birth our own fire.

Today, many women and men are returning to matriarchal philosophy and honoring the Goddess energy found in all living beings. The Goddess is the Divine Creative Force; our planet itself is a living, breathing, birthing entity. Due to the fact that we, as women, have the ability to give birth, we are inherent vessels of this Creative Force. Whether or not we become physical birth mothers, we are potential bearers of the spirit and have instinctual knowledge of the natural world. Our biological rhythms are manifested from this instinct; our capability to give birth and raise children is mirrored in the Earth's own fertility. Our menstrual cycles, when unaffected by stress, poor health, or certain methods of birth control, are akin to the moon's monthly orbit.

With this gift comes a great responsibility to nourish not only ourselves but others with our spiritual power; spiritual power does not mean *power over* but reaching our fullest potential in this lifetime. It is my belief that the Sacred Feminine inside each of us must be cultivated the same way we cultivate our careers, families, and relationships. Walking in Goddess Consciousness means being our truest selves.

Feminine inner beauty, enthusiasm, passion, and wisdom are stronger than any weapon. At the heart of the most vehement storm there is stillness. True femininity is the same. Walking in Goddess Consciousness means acting *from this center*. We are each a living link in the great chain of being. When we deprive the world of our abilities, no matter how small, we are not fulfilling our unique purpose as women. When we fail to invest in our own worth out of fear of failure or when we envy another "link" in the chain, we waste our precious potential that is greatly needed somewhere in the grand scheme of things. The creative force is the life force. The same force that compels two people to make love is the same force that beckons the artist to the easel and the seeker to Deity. It is all the same energy with different expression. When we fail to express ourselves fully, we compromise the life force. In turn, our connection to the Source is severed. Meditation, the act of finding the still center within, can help mend this connection.

Meditation has profound effects on the physical and emotional bodies. Medical researchers are beginning to recognize the benefits of meditation as well as prayer. Unfortunately, meditation is often seen as mysterious and tedious. Many of us try meditation in one form or another but still cannot find that elusive peace; each of us is different and so are our spiritual needs. One size does not fit all.

I'd like to invite you to use the paintings in this book for contemplation, observation, affirmation, and above all, quiet visual meditation; I invite you to spend time with your own feminine spirit and find your own Goddess Self just beneath the surface of your busy life.

May you make beautiful discoveries. Be free!

Earth Mother

Nature is my Mother; she is the artist who colored my eyes, the sculptor who molded my body. Her orchards and fields sustain my very existence, and her whimsical beauty feeds my soul. Where else would I find my true Self but in her?

Goddess of the Heavens

Drink from the deep, my Soul; taste the silver of its surface.

Fly! Fly the speed of stillness…

Wise Woman

**Deep in the recesses of my being, I have all of the answers; I only have to remember:
I am a child of the Goddess. All will be well. I trust the obstacles that point my path
in another direction.**

Angel of Renewal

Spring keeps her promise; trees bud back to life, deserts burst into bloom, the thirsty river overflows with rain—I am no different. In this moment, I ask for and receive complete renewal and healing where it is needed.

Infinity

At any given moment, I choose to be in the eye of the storm; chaos does not penetrate my Center.

Peace is possible.

Priestess of Beauty

Everything I touch turns to beauty; experiences, emotions, and dreams make up the unique palette of my life.

Each hour, each choice, each intention is a brush stroke.

Angel of New Beginnings

The past is finished; the future is unborn.

This hour, poised between my fingertips,

is unblemished and infinite with possibility.

I inhale the sweet air of new beginnings.

Dark Night of the Soul

When I cannot see the way ahead or understand the way I have come,

I light a single candle and ask to be able to trust the dark; every dark night of the soul has a dawn.

Rainbride

Tears are the waters of the Soul. Women's tears, like ancient

sacred springs, cleanse what is no longer needed.

My heart opens to blessed, healing rain.

17

Angel of Letting Go

Dreams, loves, ideals, selves, circumstances…sometimes outgrown;

necessary but filled with pain—the letting go.

I release all that no longer contributes to my evolution.

Muse

I am a creator,

a vessel for the Feminine Creative Force.

Thoughts and words are energy.

I am creating the life I want.

Gestation

In the heart of the rose, I wait for my hour of blooming;

not a moment too soon or too late,

fruition comes with Divine Timing.

Magdalene of the Mysteries

Beneath the dusts of time, my spirit remembers its lineage;

woman Priestesses, Healers, and Teachers

have come before me. Their wisdom flows in my DNA.

In the Garden of the Goddess

Soul of amber, breath of jasmine, I am adorned and satiated with abundance;

I want for nothing here, here in the oasis of Now.

Goddess Moon

Sister-Mother Moon, I feel the cycle of your eternal rhythm in my body and being. You inspire me to have the courage to celebrate my own brilliance and to acknowledge my own darkness.

Artemis of the Wilds

I run with the Maiden of the wilderness, ever-youthful,

ever unto Myself, sacrificing my well-being for no humanmade ideal.

I choose to be free.

Hekate of the Crossroads

In the depths of consciousness, I honor the all-knowing Crone,

the eternal magic of divine knowledge. When I stand at the crossroads,

I trust the compass of my heart.

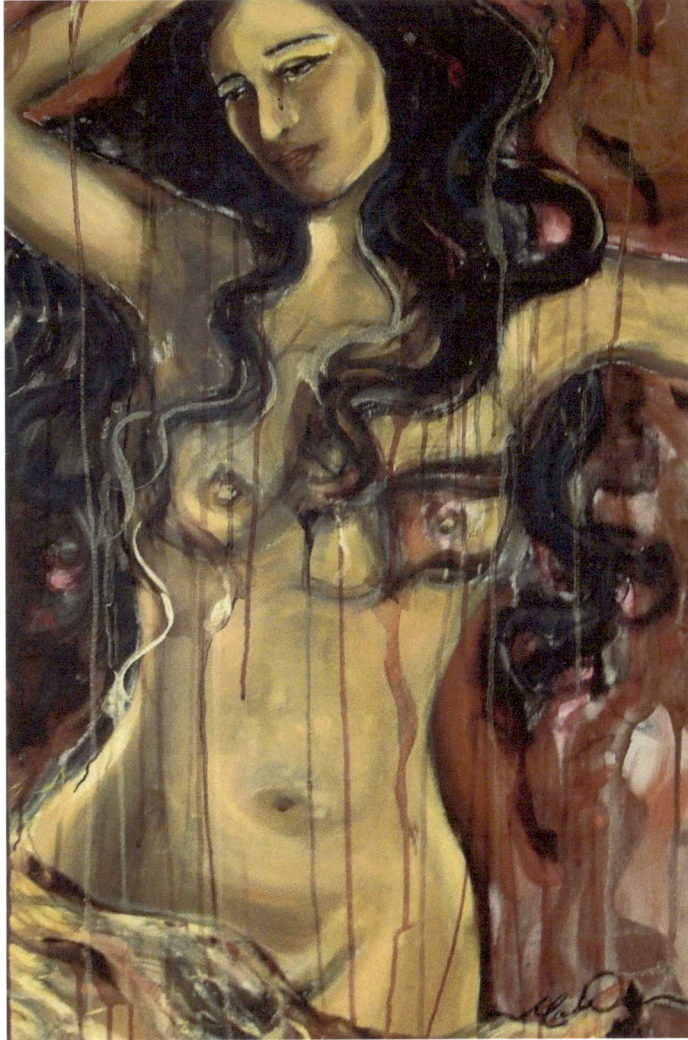

Dance of Kali

Every second in the dance of Life…somewhere, a birth…somewhere, a death;

even in my own body, the constancy of cells changing from one state to another.

Today I trust that every ending will birth a beginning.

Shakti

I ignite the fire of my own enlightenment; there is truth in all things, all ways, all encounters. I blaze in my Goddess-potential, in my sensuality, in my perfect imperfection.

Eve of Creation

I swim through the cosmos of my imaginings, creating worlds

and universes within.

I birth a new self no one has ever seen before.

Drought's End

I rejoice in possibility.

Deva

Deep in the flower's perfection, the leaf's jeweled green,

I honor the life force pulsing beneath

the surface.

The Music of my Soul

Like the seasons, I have my own rhythms, my own symphony of moods;

in the spotlight of my destiny, I dance to the music of my soul.

The Shadow Self

Roots, the dark side of the moon, and rocks beneath rapids exist in dark solitude…so too fears, unspoken hungers, and memories.

Here in this safety, I acknowledge the shadows I keep imprisoned.

Night Angel

Blessed peace, I welcome you.

Blessed peace, I honor you.

Blessed peace, I am safe beneath your wings.

Forgiveness

Forgiveness… one second, one hour, one day at a time.

Protection

I am protected in the womb of the Eternal Mother.

Sybil

The winds stir or cease at my command; I stand in a circle of fire.

Into the tempest I send prayers for the highest good.

It is done. Blessed Be. Amen.

Summer's Turning...Autumn's First Leaf

Between black and white—gray.

Between passionate youth and quiet wisdom—midlife.

Between day and night—twilight.

I honor the sacred doorways of In-Between.

Moonrise

Beneath the moon, I offer my humility

and my gratitude for the beauty of the Earth

reflected in my eyes.

About the Artist

Marlaina Donato received her first painting commission at age 16, but art did not become a dedication until her mid-20s. This spark of inspiration coincided with Marlaina's passionate and growing interest in women's studies and ancient feminine mysticism. Drawing upon a deep well of cultural mythology, Christian Gnosticism, and the wisdom of the natural world, Marlaina focused her brush on visionary art and Goddess paintings.

She is also an artist of fine art and abstracts. She is self-taught and specializes in water-based media and pure pigment dry pastel. Marlaina's solo exhibits in Pennsylvania, Virginia, and New Jersey have also included her art photography and multimedia works. She has donated her work to support Public Television.

Marlaina is the author of several books including Naked Soul (Llewellyn,1998) A Brief Infinity, The Silver Ladder, Hollow Bread, and Broken Jar. She teaches women's meditation classes and co-facilitates women's Goddess day retreats. She and her beloved husband Joe live in rural New Jersey with their canine muse Noah. Contact: www.marlainadonato.com

Paintings

1. *Earth Mother* Copyright 1997 Marlaina Donato (acrylic on board)
2. *Goddess of the Heavens* Copyright 1996 Marlaina Donato (acrylic on board)
3. *Wise Woman* Copyright 2001 Marlaina Donato (pastel on board)
4. *Angel of Renewal* Copyright 2009 Marlaina Donato (pastel on paper)
5. *Infinity* Copyright 1992, 2011 Marlaina Donato (pastel on board)
6. *Priestess of Beauty* Copyright 1996 Marlaina Donato (pastel on board)
7. *Angel of New Beginnings* Copyright 2009 Marlaina Donato (pastel on paper)
8. *Dark Night of the Soul* Copyright 2003 Marlaina Donato (acrylic on canvas)
9. *Rainbride* Copyright 1996 Marlaina Donato (acrylic on board)
10. *Angel of Letting Go* Copyright 2008 Marlaina Donato (acrylic on canvas)
11. *Muse* Copyright 2006 Marlaina Donato (acrylic on canvas)
12. *Gestation* Copyright 2008 Marlaina Donato (acrylic on canvas)
13. *Magdalene of the Mysteries* 1 Copyright 2008 (acrylic on canvas)
                                                      2 Copyright 2003 (acrylic on canvas)
14. *In the Garden of the Goddess* Copyright 2006 Marlaina Donato (acrylic on canvas)
15. *Goddess Moon* 1 Copyright 2006 Marlaina Donato (acrylic on canvas)
                                2 Copyright 2012 Marlaina Donato (acrylic on canvas)
16. *Artemis of the Wilds* Copyright 1998 Marlaina Donato (mixed media on canvas board)
17. *Hekate of the Crossroads* Copyright 1998 Marlaina Donato (mixed media on canvas board)
18. *Dance of Kali* Copyright 2005 Marlaina Donato (acrylic on canvas)
19. *Shakti* Copyright 1996 Marlaina Donato (acrylic on board)
20. *Eve of Creation* Copyright 2000 Marlaina Donato (acrylic on board)
21. *Drought's End* Copyright 2006 Marlaina Donato (acrylic on canvas)
22. *Deva* Copyright 2009 Marlaina Donato (pastel on paper)
23. *The Music of my Soul* Copyright 2008 Marlaina Donato (acrylic on canvas)
24. *Night Angel* Copyright 2008 Marlaina Donato (acrylic on canvas)

25. *Forgiveness* Copyright 1995 Marlaina Donato (pastel on board)
26. *Protection* Copyright 2009 Marlaina Donato (pastel on paper)
27. *Sybil* Copyright 2005 Marlaina Donato (acrylic on canvas)
28. *Summer's Turning…Autumn's First Leaf* Copyright 2008 Marlaina Donato (acrylic on canvas)
29. *Moonrise* Copyright 2011 Marlaina Donato (pastel on paper)

Bibliography

Redmond, Layne. When the Drummers Were Women. NY,NY: Three Rivers Press, 1997

Walker, Barbara. The Woman's Encyclopedia of Myth and Secrets. San Francisco, CA: Harper and Row, 1983